Life in the Arctic

T0372100

by Anne Giulieri

The Arctic

The Arctic is a very cold place on *Earth*.
It is at the top of Earth near the *North Pole*.
The Arctic is a very big place.

Most of the Arctic
is made up of water.
Some of the water is *frozen*.
Water that is frozen in the
Arctic Ocean is called sea ice.

The Arctic also has thick ice that covers land.
This ice moves slowly.
When the ice breaks off into the ocean,
it is called an *iceberg*.
All of this ice can be covered in snow.

People

People have lived in the Arctic for a very long time.
People in the Arctic hunt and fish.
They know how to stay safe from the cold.

Everyone who lives in the Arctic needs
to wear clothes that protect them from the cold.
People have to put on
coats, boots and hats
when they go outside.

The buildings in the Arctic keep people warm and safe.

People go from place to place on sleds and *snowmobiles*.

They also go on snow trucks and snow *skis*.

This helps them to go through snow and over the ice.

Day and night

The Arctic has summer and winter.
In summer it is light.
In winter it is dark.

In summer it's light most of the time.

There are even times when the sun does not *set*.

When the sun does not go down, it never gets dark.

This is called the *midnight* sun.

Even when it is not dark at bedtime,

children still need to go to sleep.

People in the Arctic have to sleep

when it is light outside!

Winter

In winter it is dark most of the time.

There are times when the sun does not come up at all.

When the sun does not come up, it never gets light.

This is called *polar* night.

On very dark days, people still work and go to school.

Street lights stay on during the day.

This helps people to see where they are walking or driving.

The children go outside even when it is cold and snowing.

In some places, children ride sleds to school.

Some schools have sled racks instead of bike racks.

Plants

The Arctic can sometimes look
like it does not have plants.
But it does.
You just have to look for them.

Plants that grow in the Arctic are small.

They have small leaves and can grow under snow.

There are also small *bushes* that grow in the Arctic.

There are some parts of the Arctic that have small trees.

Animals

There are many animals in the Arctic, too.

Many of the animals are big.

They also have a lot of *fur*.

They can also have fat called *blubber* under their skin.

This helps them to stay warm.

polar bear

Some animals that live in the Arctic are white.
Polar bears, arctic foxes and snowy owls
are the colour of snow.
This helps to keep them safe.

arctic fox

snowy owl

The cold Arctic is home to many people, plants and animals. They live, work and play in the snowy Arctic.

Picture glossary

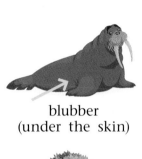
blubber
(under the skin)

frozen

midnight

set

bushes

fur

North Pole

skis

Earth

iceberg

polar

snowmobiles